Emile Zola

by

JEAN-ALBERT BÉDÉ

Columbia University Press

NEW YORK & LONDON 1974

COLUMBIA ESSAYS ON MODERN WRITERS
is a series of critical studies of English,
Continental, and other writers whose works are of contemporary
artistic and intellectual significance.

Editor

George Stade

Advisory Editors

Jacques Barzun   W. T. H. Jackson   Joseph A. Mazzeo

Emile Zola is Number 69 of the series

JEAN-ALBERT BÉDÉ
a native of France, was Professor of French
at Columbia University from 1937 to 1971.
At the time of his retirement he held
the Blanche W. Knopf chair of French literature.
A former general editor of the *Romanic Review,*
he is now engaged in revising the
Columbia Dictionary of Modern European Literatures
and editing the two nineteenth-century
volumes of the *Critical Bibliography
of French Literature* ("Cabeen Bibliography").

Library of Congress Cataloging in Publication Data

Bédé, Jean Albert.
  Emile Zola.

  (Columbia essays on modern writers, no. 69)
Bibliography: p. 48
1. Zola, Émile, 1840–1902 — Criticism and interpreta-
tion. I. Series.
PQ2538.B4   843'.8   74-1158
ISBN 0-231-02977-2

Emile Zola

Emile Zola, a "modern writer"? The case, no doubt, is debatable. His birth on April 2, 1840, harks back to the days of Louis-Philippe, king of the French. Even the fact that, but for a freak of fate, he could have witnessed World War I does not qualify him, at least beyond dispute, as a forerunner of modern trends. Significantly enough, a collection of essays and testimonials, entitled *Présence de Zola,* appeared in 1953 under the signatures of older devotees only. Thomas Mann headed the list, and his opening sentence, ringing like an epigraph to the entire volume, praised Zola as an exemplar . . . of the nineteenth century.

What are, then, Zola's titles to the exceptional treatment he is receiving nevertheless, in and out of France, as a living figure?

Obviously, I daresay overwhelmingly, the part he played in the Dreyfus Affair constitutes a prime factor. Nowadays, to a surprising number of moderately cultured people, those exotic syllables, Zola, spell courage and decency. The paunchy, myopic man with the beribboned pince-nez, never a shining knight in his physical appearance, has achieved the recognition Anatole France promised him as "a moment of the conscience of mankind." This, be it noted, is a posthumous, indeed comparatively recent, development. No one should suppose, for instance, that the transfer of Zola's remains to the Panthéon (1908), which followed shortly upon the rehabilitation of Captain Dreyfus, united friends and foes in at least a display of esteem for the dead man's character. Far from it! Contrived as a political gesture by the then Premier (none other than Zola's old com-

[3]

rade-in-arms, Georges Clemenceau), the ceremony was marred by vociferous protests from the rightist faction and by an attempt on the life of Dreyfus himself. It is, in fact, no exaggeration to say that only the trials of World War II rid Zola's name of its former, divisive virulence.

In the United States, too, Zola was a beneficiary of World War II or of events that led to it. For a long time his American fortunes had pursued a wholly predictable course. When Balzac ceased to be anathema to self-respecting families, Zola replaced him as the main proponent of Gallic materialism and godlessness —and as purveyor of smut extraordinary. To be sure, he, unlike Balzac, had earned a similar reputation at home: Barbey d'Aurevilly dubbed him "the Michelangelo of the gutter"; François Mauriac vividly recalled how his parents referred to chamber pots as "the zolas." The French, however, proved to be lusty customers of whatever the devil had to offer, whereas the American public, such as it was, labored under a sense of guilt. As late as 1927, Ernest A. Boyd depicted Zola in the garb of the Antichrist. Then, on the eve of the war, linked, it would seem, to a feeling of revulsion against Hitler's malevolence, especially against his persecution of the Jews, a dramatic change occurred: Hollywood, *mirabile dictu,* was responsible for it. Woefully inaccurate in its detail, but saved by the grace of Paul Muni's performance, a screen version of Zola's life lifted him bodily from the realm of the damned into that of the heroes of thought. The Dreyfus Affair supplied the necessary pathos, and, incidentally, enough "punchlines" were delivered to bruise the sensitivities of the French government, whose censors banned the film for twenty years and then insisted on substantial cuts.

Zola was not born a fighter: he molded himself into one. As a youth he had displayed escapist traits which were indicative

[4]

of a thoroughly romantic make-up. Later he took his espousal of "naturalism" to represent a repudiation of those early tendencies. Still later, however, he himself entertained few illusions that, on escaping escapism, he had uprooted his romanticism as well.

The poet in him came from the South, unmistakably. There remained throughout, to Zola's literary stance, a wordy, almost rhetorical touch which bespoke its Mediterranean origins. Until he "went up" to Paris—to stay and to struggle—the accident of his birth in the capital weighed but lightly against the fifteen formative years (1843–58) that he spent, for the most part, at Aix-en-Provence. Nor do his near-Parisian roots on the maternal side alter the picture significantly. When, at the age of twenty, Emilie Aubert married forty-four-year-old François Zola, a native Dalmatian, half-Italian and half-Greek, she, to all practical purposes, entered the typically Southern world of her husband.

A civil engineer of some merit, but prone to embark upon highly speculative ventures, the elder Zola died in 1847, leaving his family in dire financial straits. He was still a citizen of Venice. So was young Emile, according to French law, until he became of age and could apply for naturalization papers. Some day his political enemies would brand him a *métèque* (a foreigner, an interloper)—about the worst insult in their vocabulary.

The next ten years tell a tale of endless court battles fought by François Zola's widow to stem the tide of oncoming ruin and ensure a proper education for her son. When the boy finally entered secondary school, he was late in his studies and inordinately shy. Luck had it, however, that he came under the protective wing of two older schoolmates, the sons of well-established local families, one of whom, Paul Cézanne, was also destined to fame as an artist. For several years, on Sundays and holidays, the three companions did roam the countryside, drinking in the poetry of nature along with that of their favorite poets. Hugo was their first god, soon joined, then eclipsed, by Alfred de Musset. Musset, the nonchalant roué par excellence, was already on his way to the strange destiny that made him a healer of adolescent pangs, adept at dissolving them into wisps of idealized love. Chalk him up, paradoxical though it may seem, as Zola's original master and prompter. Musset it was who "taught me how to weep"—delicious tears, of course, while waiting for bitter ones. Musset it was who peopled the sun-drenched, lavender-scented solitudes of Provence with a number of "love-fairies," all to become one, in due time, as the imaginary dedicatee of the *Contes à Ninon.*

There is today, with increasing frequency, another, a tragic side to Provençal inspiration. The murderous sun and wind, and the primitive passions they foster, supply the underlying theme of many a novel by Jean Giono, Thyde Monnier, or Henri Bosco. Zola may have shown the way in some passages of *Les Rougon-Macquart;* but, as a general rule, I cannot see that he forged a specific link between the greed of his Provençal creatures and the ruggedness of their habitat. His one novel of the soil has the plenteous Beauce for its locale. The Rougons are small-town products. They, and the Macquarts, too, fall prey to the mistral, Provence's ruling wind, only in the sense that modern conditions make it, spiritually speaking, a germ-carrier, laden with the miasmas of political intrigue and urbanized civilization. All in all, Zola's vision of Provence remained that of an earthly paradise, perhaps lost forever, which he drew from limbo on at least one occasion when he wanted to conjure up a tableau of luxuriant love amidst the complicities of Nature. I refer, of course, to that fantastic creation of his—the sheltered, impossibly huge park in *La Faute de l'abbé Mouret* (The Transgression of Abbé Mouret), where the hero and his child-mistress play Adam and Eve, and the name of which, aptly enough, happens to be "le Paradou."

[6]

By 1858 Mme Zola moved to Paris in search of work and assistance. Emile, for his part, entered the Lycée Saint-Louis, a badly confused youth whose scholastic averages fell precipitously. At nineteen, in his kind of situation, there was no recourse except to quit school and look for employment. He found none, or none that mattered, until February, 1862, when he became a shipping clerk in the publishing firm of Hachette & Co. A biographical sketch, written at a later date for the benefit of Alphonse Daudet, reads in part: "The years 1860 and 1861, abominable. Not a penny to my name, literally. Whole days without food. . . . Sort of happy, nevertheless. Interminable walks across Paris, especially along the quays, which I adored." Note this last: the Siren had sung her song, the poor devil was hopelessly smitten.

It is not easy to measure the impact of Paris on Zola's imagination. Paris, to him personally, became the crucible of every manly experience, intellectual as well as emotional. This accounted for still another romantic relationship, though far less elemental, hence far less elementary, than had been his with Provence. Where dream meets reality, the clash is bound to have complex reverberations. It took Zola a lifetime to sort his feelings in the matter. The late novel which bears Paris's name will restore her to her pristine splendor as the City of Light. Midway through the novelist's career, she will stand again and again in the image of the Modern Metropolis, whose brazen law crushes or degrades human values. Yet, on other occasions, the perspective appears to reverse itself: Paris, then, emerges as a victim, perhaps the most pitiable of them all, her soul and body violated by the ruffians of the Second Empire. Just now, to the famished newcomer in his garret, she is little more than a temptress whose cruel whims fill him with alternate moods of despair and anger.

When chance contacts in the house of Hachette finally enabled Zola to break into print, his sparse readers were treated to a battle royal between the "Provençal," or Musset-in-pink, and the

[7]

"Parisian," or Musset-in-black, brands of emotionalism. The *Contes à Ninon* (Tales for Ninon, 1864), his maiden effort, fairly dripped with maudlin sentimentality; and, believe it or not, this vein did not dry out for ten more years (*Nouveaux Contes à Ninon,* 1874). Dark, drab, desolate romanticism, on the other hand, informed *La Confession de Claude,* Zola's earliest full-length novel (1865). This story of bohemian life, told in the first person, with strong autobiographical overtones, recounted a young man's pathetic attempts at redeeming both the prostitute who had initiated him and himself in the process. But stark though they were, and reminiscent of Musset's *Confession d'un enfant du siècle* (Confession of a Child of the Century), Claude's juvenile effusions ended on the hopeful note—possibly an echo from Hugo's *Les Misérables* (1862)—that whoever "tears the fabric of the night" may "hasten the slow and majestic rise of the day." Even His Imperial Majesty's Prosecutor General, who frowned at the vividness of some of the scenes, had to concede that the book on the whole did not offend public morality.

Late in 1865, Zola—never a philanderer, by the way—entered into a serious affair with Gabrielle-Alexandrine Meley, whom he was to marry in 1870. Shortly afterwards (January, 1866) he resigned from his job in order to embark upon a journalistic career. This was a calculated risk. Potentially at any rate, it meant money—the sinew of independence. It also meant a tribune, an audience, an intoxicating sense of power.

Zola left us an enormous legacy of newspaper and magazine articles. Those he collected (nine volumes in all) represent only a fraction of his output. Any but the briefest comments thereon would cause the present essay to burst at the seams. Let it be clear, however, that if poetry expressed Zola's first nature, then journalism became his second. The one tended to abstract him from the world, the other brought him back with a vengeance. Literary chronicler, art critic, political columnist, social reporter,

[8]

he achieved identification with his times through this journalistic ubiquity. He likewise discovered the advantages of pre-publishing his novels in serialized form and, initially at least, was not above serving up a couple of potboilers (*Le Voeu d'une morte* [A Dead Woman's Vow], 1866; *Les Mystères de Marseille,* 1867). All in all, nevertheless, he took his responsibilities most zealously. Unlike Flaubert or the Goncourts, he did not mind "dirtying his hands" in the give-and-take of public controversy: so much so that even his fictional work may be said—not the least bit disparagingly—to be journalistic in essence. By divesting the word of its ephemeral connotations, only to retain what journalism meant to him *as a vehicle,* one arrives at a fair understanding of Zola's mental processes. Half of his writings, novels included, ring in some *vérité en marche*—as did, specifically, his last campaign in Clemenceau's newspaper, *L'Aurore.* And surely, *J'accuse* would make a handsome caption for the other half.

It is fitting to remark at this point that Zola, fervent crusader though he was, never evinced an interest in active politics, never carried a "party card," never courted elective office, never spoke on the issues in anyone's name save his own. Even *J'accuse,* with its stress on the first person, was to be the public utterance of a private citizen. Its author, in other terms, was basically the same man whose *Confession de Claude* had romantically asserted the individual's prerogative to cry out his feelings *(vivre tout haut).* The same man who, at the age of twenty-six (1866), published his first collection of critical essays as *Mes haines*— *my* hatreds—and another (on the annual Art Exhibition) under the title of *Mon Salon.* As his outlook steadily widened, running the gamut from emotional to aesthetic to social experience, so did, in fact, his need for self-expression.

There is every reason to suppose that Zola's political sympathies, at the outset of his career, were already oriented to the

[9]

left. Yet, his concept of the creative artist as supreme among individuals threatened to make a shambles of whatever democratic principles he may have had. Next to the conservative pundits, whose fiats and taboos stifled the progress of art, *hoi polloi* —obtuse, sheeplike, fainthearted—were the target of his contempt: for it was they who recoiled at the boldness of the Goncourt brothers' *Germinie Lacerteux* or burst out laughing before a Manet canvas. But where do you draw the line between the people as common people and what is called "the public"? Zola —the young Zola—did not quite know and did not care: "Frankly," he averred, "I would sacrifice humanity to the artist." By much the same token, he rebuked Hippolyte Taine himself, who submerged the artist under the mechanical forces that govern the world. As if an invention counted for anything outside of the inventor; as if a work of art were not "a corner of nature reflected through the author's temperament"! This oft-quoted formula recurs three times in *Mes haines* and *Mon Salon,* then, rather startlingly, after a nine-year interval, in a study on Dumas *fils.* By that time (1875) Zola was an avowed disciple of Taine and fast becoming a social-minded writer. Paradox, or contradiction? Neither, I venture to say. He was henceforth reasonably satisfied that he could reconcile a fiercely personalized stance with the exigencies of humanitarian concern. He likewise saw himself as temperamentally suited to become a surveyor of temperaments.

The word "temperament" plainly belongs to the vocabulary of psycho-physiology. It has always been reminiscent of Galen's old theory of humors. In the late eighteenth and early nineteenth centuries the Idéologues used it, or reasonable equivalents, to counteract and dispel the animistic implications of the word "character." When Zola happened on the scene, their influence had been running through two separate channels. The straighter current had carried far enough to produce Taine's massive, monistic-mechanistic philosophy and, of late, to receive Darwin's powerful contribution. On the other hand, the more circuitous romantic route had allowed for a great deal of compromise. Romantic writers were not hard-core materialists and conceived of a spiritual world over, above, and in conjunction with that of physical necessity. The latter was not ignored, however, and claimed an ever-growing share of their attention. Jules Michelet, whose impact on the young Zola looms uncommonly large, made almost a fetish of physiological causes in his *Tableau de la France* and his disquisitions on *La Femme* and *L'Amour*. Nor could it be denied that, from Balzac's *Comédie humaine* to the Goncourts' *Germinie Lacerteux,* by way of *Madame Bovary,* the novel crystallized along increasingly "clinical" lines. By 1866, the gap was about to close between harder and softer determinists—and Zola seemed predestined to close it. How and how much he hovered on the threshold of decision may be gathered from the following pronouncement—wherein, incidentally, he stumbled on a future title of his: "What we do nowadays is take a *bête humaine* and study him *within the margin of freedom* left him by his environment" (italics mine).

The protagonists of Zola's next two novels—*Thérèse Raquin* (1867) and *Madeleine Férat* (1868)—are indeed human brutes, swayed by the "fatalities" of their nerves, blood, and flesh. It matters little that Thérèse and Laurent end as criminals, whereas Madeleine and Guillaume certainly do not. Both stories are "autopsies" in Zola's words, "case studies" in our own—one verging on the exceptional and the other falling squarely into it.

Case number one arises from a trite enough "triangle" situation. Thérèse's pitifully inadequate husband sealed his doom when he brought his friend, Laurent, into the family circle. In the course of a boat ride wife and lover drown him and camouflage the deed as an accident. A kind of visceral revulsion (about the only "remorse" soulless creatures can feel) grips them when the body is recovered from the Seine and they are called upon to identify it. The corpse will keep intruding, in a quasi-physical way, upon the murderers' days and nights—until, finally, they commit suicide under the very eyes of the victim's paralyzed mother, who has known their secret for some time and gloats mutely over their demise.

Case number two purported to illustrate the "law" enunciated in Michelet's book *L'Amour,* to the effect that he who impregnates or even merely possesses a virgin remains her "spouse" for all time. Nothing whatever may erase the original imprint: so much so that children by a second husband are likely to resemble the first. Faithful to the script, Zola drags Madeleine through the whole, harrowing experience, and makes doubly sure of the result by having her conceive in the room she once shared with her lover. The macabre denouement, as improbable as the episodes that led to it, brings death to the child, suicide to Madeleine, and insanity to the father.

There is some unfairness in pooling together the awkwardly contrived machine that is *Madeleine Férat* and a near-masterpiece such as *Thérèse Raquin.* Ideologically, however, they belong to the same transitional period and conceal a residue of caution beneath their outward boldness. True enough, the "margin of freedom" enjoyed by Zola's characters had shrunk to practically nil. True again, he now (for the first time) called himself a "naturalist writer" and flaunted, as an epigraph to the second printing of *Thérèse Raquin,* Taine's famous dictum: "Vice and virtue are products like vitriol and sugar." Yet, it is symptomatic that, even then, he paid little heed to the *race,* or heredity, ingredient which surely, to a simon-pure physiologist, must be paramount in controlling the chemistry of temperaments. Neither story enlightens us very much as to the antecedents of the dramatis personae. Where they are concerned the word "prod-

[12]

uct" does not point to a definite hereditary legacy. Slaves they are, but to the primordial instincts that rule the animal kingdom at large, and then, to *moment* and *milieu* in the narrowest sense —namely, to the circumstances of time and place which throw them together.

Not until the winter months of 1868–69 was the last piece of the puzzle allowed to fall into position. The hard-driving novelist spent part of that time poring over medical books, among them a *Traité philosophique et physiologique de l'hérédité naturelle*, by Dr. Prosper Lucas (2 vols., 1847–50). Its author assumed an air of authority—mostly unwarranted—which may or may not have deceived Zola into endorsing his thoroughly deterministic conclusions. That he appropriated those is, of course, a matter of record; but he permitted himself an aside or two which leave some doubt as to the depth of his conviction. One needs a hypothesis, he reflected, "whether or not it is accepted as indisputably true." Or again: "Let me take a philosophical prop, for the sake . . . of connecting my books with one another. Materialism may be the best bet, for it believes in forces that will require no explaining." Quite refreshing, this dash of humor (one hopes it *is* humor), as Zola braces himself for the grim, twenty-five-year exertion that will produce *Les Rougon-Macquart.*

Unlike Balzac, who began with hardly any preconceptions at all, then codified his system some twelve years and one hundred works later, Zola, the engineer's son, drew the most elaborate blueprints, only to depart from them, consciously or not, on many occasions. At least the substance of his voluminous preliminary notes may readily be found in modern editions and monographs; but whoever is unable to wade through them will find a substitute of sorts in *Le Docteur Pascal,* the last novel in the series (1893), part of which comprises a recapitulation and interpretation of what has gone on before. The author achieved

[13]

this perilously didactic purpose by creating one member of the Rougon tribe with whom he could identify. At his death in 1873, Dr. Pascal Rougon is supposed to have left behind him an impressive "natural and social history of his family under the Second Empire"—in other terms, right down to its subtitle, a dummy replica of *Les Rougon-Macquart.* A poetic license is involved here, whereby the good doctor, revived in print twenty years after his official demise, surveys his creator's progress over the intervening decades and, more significantly still, endorses the conscientious qualms and modified viewpoints that such a long travail necessarily entailed.

For the benefit of his niece and pupil, Clotilde, Pascal displays his pride and joy—the family tree that Zola had drawn at a very early stage, no later than 1869 or 1870, then made public, in quasi-final form, as an appendix to *Une page d'amour* (A Love Story, 1878). Rooted in Plassans (i.e., Aix-en-Provence), the "stump" is represented by Adélaïde Rougon, née Fouque, still alive in 1872 at the age of one hundred and four, but neurotic from birth and definitely insane since 1851. She had borne three children: one, Pierre, by her husband, a hard-working gardener; two, Ursule and Antoine, by her lover, a disreputable smuggler named Macquart. The three branches had proliferated, even becoming knotted through the marriage of François Mouret, Ursule's son, to Marthe Rougon, Pierre's daughter. By 1872 Adélaïde's descendants number about thirty. All exemplify in varying degree "the laws of nerve and blood irregularities which as the result of a primal organic lesion break out among members of a family."

An obedient disciple of Prosper Lucas, Pascal has adopted his nomenclature of hereditary components and done "as scientific a job as possible" of apportioning them in each and every case. Yet, he expresses reservations that were Zola's in 1893 but may not have been his at the outset. Who can ever hope not to miss an important collateral contribution? Most of all, how much credit should be given an infant discipline which, temporarily at least, straddles the frontier between poetry and science proper?

Poets walk as pioneers, in the vanguard; oftentimes they discover virgin territory and point to forthcoming answers. *There* lies a margin all their own—that which separates the truth already conquered, already definitive, from the unknown whence will be extracted the truth of tomorrow. . . . What an immense fresco stands to be painted, what a colossal human comedy or tragedy awaits its writer, in the form of heredity—the very Genesis, you might say, of families, societies, and the entire world!

Granted, by now, that heredity provides the theme for all human manifestations, natural and instinctive, the products of which we call virtues and vices. But understood, too, that milieu and moment play the variations. Milieu and moment rise henceforth to their full stature as a spatial and temporal climate—a living stage of Darwinian proportions, made to order for the strong, treacherous to the weak: all the more so, in modern times, as it keeps shifting at an accelerated pace. The Rougon-Macquart story, Pascal muses,

epitomizes that of the Second Empire from Louis-Napoleon's coup d'état to the Sedan defeat. . . . Our folk issued from the people; they spread all over contemporary society; they invaded all fields, carried, as it were, on the tidal wave of present-day cravings.

Ambivalent feelings—again the later Zola's feelings—pervade this verdict. Still very much to the fore, in 1893, is his detestation of an era when materialistic principles (not bad in themselves: how could they be, to a materialist?) became perverted at the hands of schemers, speculators, and social climbers. Yet, he has the doctor contending that civilization is better than the sum of its parts—that the life current, even as it crosses a wasteland of dregs and scoria, retains its inherent majesty and will purge itself in due time.

[15]

Such buoyant hopes may have had their germ in Zola's attitude toward the Franco-Prussian war. Exempt from conscription as a widow's son, he spent most of the wartime months in unoccupied southern France. Thus was he spared the permanent scars that closer experience inflicted upon some of his future disciples (Maupassant, Huysmans, etc.), causing them to wallow in stark pessimism and think of themselves as a "lost generation." What is more, the swift collapse of the regime presented him with a providential finis to his contemplated saga. Until then, the fortunes of the Rougon-Macquart stood open-ended, so to speak, and no Tarpeian rock could clearly be seen near the Capitol. As Fate took a hand, Zola shed a tear for the innocent but welcomed the punishment visited upon the guilty. Shocking or not, his concept of war—of that particular war—was in the biblical tradition of Joseph de Maistre. At the outbreak of hostilities, a violent article of his had exhorted "fifty thousand French soldiers on the bank of the Rhine" to refuse to fight for the imperial government. Come the Sedan capitulation and the subsequent overthrow of that government, he viewed the catastrophe as a purifying process, still unspeakably cruel in its immediate repercussions, yet therapeutic in the long run.

Seven novels span a first period, 1871–77, through which the author tried his formula upon a long-reluctant public. Both in form and in substance, this sub-cycle exhibits characteristics that faded toward the end.

Initially at least, the Rougons dominated the scene. They enjoyed, over the Macquarts, the advantage of legitimacy; and with it, a driving spirit, a native shrewdness, that their underprivileged cousins did not possess in equal proportion. *La Fortune des Rougon* (volume one of the series, written before the war, published in 1871), *La Conquête de Plassans* (volume four, 1874), and *Son Excellence Eugène Rougon* (volume six, 1876)

[16]

show Pierre Rougon's eldest son, Eugène, masterminding his
family into a position of commanding local power and himself
into the highest of state functions. In this particular group the
first novel is easily the best; but no small interest attaches to
Zola's recital of the Excellency's career, modeled in large part
after that of Eugène Rouher, Napoleon III's Minister of State
for seven years. Its merit lies in the nugget of universal truth
that Zola managed to extract from his consideration of modern
"machine politics" and "government by cronies."

Aristide, the Rougon couple's second son, takes over in *La
Curée* (The Kill; volume two, 1872). To him the lower forms of
gratification: money, women, luxury. A matter of days after the
coup d'état, he "swoops down" on Paris like a vulture. Under
the assumed name of Saccard (it would not do to embarrass
brother Eugène), he makes, loses, and recoups millions through
the wild real-estate speculations which attended Baron Hauss-
mann's program for the beautification of the capital. His second
marriage to a girl much younger than himself is a purely financial transaction which leads him to tolerate an incestuous relationship between her and his grown-up son, Maxime. The most
scabrous episodes of this liaison take place in the hothouse of
Saccard's mansion and introduce the reader to an early device
of Zola's, symbolistic in essence, which emphasizes the mimetic
influence of environment. Maxime and his stepmother literally
grow into "flowers of evil," almost indistinguishable from the
huge poisonous plants that witness and condone their vicious
disport.

Volume three in the cycle (1873) interrupted the Rougon
parade long enough to bring forward a major Macquart figure.
Savage Paris is as far as English translators ever went in rendering its title, *Le Ventre de Paris*. An early one passed it off as
The Flower and Market Girls of Paris. Flower and market girls
indeed! Lying and jutting out before us is the City's Belly—

namely, the Central Market *(les Halles),* a shining new structure (1854) at the time of the action. Smelly, oily, greasy, meaty, cheesy as you please, its opulence comes off, mimetically once again, on the shopkeepers who thrive in its shadow. This is the kingdom of the Fat, and Lisa Quenu, Antoine Macquart's elder daughter, stands very nearly enthroned as its queen. No Rougon would aspire to her kind of royalty, founded as it is on ungrateful chores and the practice of petty-bourgeois virtues. The Rougons own the law, sometimes make it, and gamble under its cover. Not so the Macquarts. Outsiders they are and misfits they remain for the most part; but the few among them who do not topple from various heights or drift aimlessly may be expected to learn the hard way about the exact price of security and respectability. Take honest Lisa, encamped in her delicatessen store, for a rare illustration of how a "reformed" Macquart is apt to turn into a pillar of society. When brother-in-law Florent, a political subversive, becomes a liability, she betrays him to the police and has him sent back to the penal colony whence he first came.

Implicit in Zola's very premises, the theme of the fall followed closely upon that of the rise and began asserting itself with *La Faute de l'abbé Mouret* (volume five, 1875). Mention has been made earlier of the walled Paradou, or Zola's version of a Provençal Garden of Eden, where young abbé Serge Mouret convalesces after an attack of brain fever and is nursed by sixteen-year-old Albine, the park attendant's niece. A love story unfolds, wringing from the author's pen a torrential but final outflow of the same metaphoric "correspondences" which ran through *La Curée* and *Le Ventre de Paris.* Albine, herself, is a flower of that paradise; from the flowers and from the trees, to whose Song of Songs her inner ear is attuned, she asks and receives "thunderous" encouragement as she leads Serge along the path of temptation; and when she realizes that she is a woman after

[18]

all, with a balance of unfulfilled desires that no vegetable, nor even unthinking animals, can possibly experience, she still wants to die as a flower among flowers, on a bed of hyacinths and tuberoses whose sweet "symphony" slowly asphyxiates her. But what of Serge's so-called transgression? It is definitely not related to the breaking of his chastity vows: for Zola views priestly celibacy as a monstrous imposition, virginity as an abnormal state, and sexual intercourse — provided it does not elude the procreative ends of nature — as the life-giving sacrament. For a clue to his meaning, one must turn once more to omniscient Dr. Pascal. The following is a portrait of Serge's uncle as he revisits the Paradou's site — long after the garden has been torn down:

He, Pascal, was a scholar, a clear-sighted man. He did not believe in an idyllic humanity living in a land of milk and honey. He saw, instead, the evils and the taints; he had spread them out, probed, catalogued them for thirty years; and all he needed was his passion for life, his reverence for the energies of life, to throw him into a perpetual joy: whence flowed his love of others, a fraternal emotion, an empathy detectable even under his rough exterior of an anatomist and the factitious impersonality of his studies.

This is Zola describing Zola as he saw himself eighteen years after the publication of *La Faute de l'abbé Mouret.* Which strands had led from it to *Germinal* and *La Terre,* which would lead further to *Les Trois villes* and *Fécondité,* were by then becoming apparent. And so was the true "error" of abbé Mouret. The Paradou had vanished like a dream. The Paradou *was* a dream. Serge, henceforth a poor parish priest, slowly dying from consumption, had been doomed to fall into the realities of the world-in-exile symbolized by the communities nearby — a world where grim, obdurate peasants, ploughing the earth and their women alike, toiled in utter blindness for the harvests of the future.

Thus far established critics had paid scant attention to Zola's

[19]

novels. *La Faute de l'abbé Mouret,* for the first time, drew some lively comment—severe as a rule and most of it denouncing this "outrage" to "the noble spiritualism of Christianity" (Barbey d'Aurevilly). But it remained for *L'Assommoir* (volume seven, 1877) to unleash a literary storm second only to the controversies which *La Terre* was to arouse ten years later.

L'Assommoir carries the reader hundreds of physical and spiritual miles from the fairylike Paradou—to a Parisian faubourg ominously called "de la Goutte d'Or" (of the Golden Drop) from what, in olden days, must have been a tavern sign. In due course the scene narrows down to one of the saloons with which the neighborhood is liberally sprinkled. Old man Colombe's establishment stays nameless: we merely know that it is an *assommoir*—a "knock-out bar"—similar to others and the epitome of them all. The feeling of epic simplification becomes reinforced through further pinpointing—this time to the evil heart of the house, the "rot-gut dispenser":

The attraction of the place was, toward the back, on the other side of an oak railing, in a glass-encased courtyard, the distilling machine working in full view of the patrons—a mess of long-necked alembics, of retorts reaching underground, a hellish kind of brewery in front of which boozing workers stood a-dreaming.

Such procedure evolved from Zola's previous uses of symbolism, but it was not the same procedure. Gone the former sense of identification and quasi-parity between actors and surroundings. As Zola developed the pattern of failure, the logic of the system compelled him to stress the ascendancy of things. He could not become more of a materialist, but he could—and did—write "of mice and men," sometimes locked in uneven combat against the forces of nature, sometimes ensnared in traps of their own making.

The pernicious powers that issue from *l'assommoir* radiate and fester like a cancer. They shatter the comparative happiness

[20]

of the Coupeau household. In the wake of a bad accident, the husband, a roofer by trade, loses his zest for work and takes to drink. The wife, Gervaise, struggles for a while, keeps her laundry-shop going, but moral decay is contagious. When Coupeau brings in Lantier, a former lover of hers, by whom she had had three children before marriage; when, under the eyes of Anna (Nana), her legitimate daughter, sordid episodes follow, her will, never too strong, breaks down completely: she in turn becomes an alcoholic and will die at forty-one, "slowly, horribly, exhausted by pain and misery." A most moving creation, this sister of Lisa Macquart's — and as pathetic, as lovable, in her defenselessness, as the matron of *les Halles* was sturdy and coldly aseptic.

A practical lesson *(de la morale en action)* according to its author, *L'Assommoir* hovered on the brink of didacticism. That it stayed clear of this pitfall redounds to Zola's eternal credit. However, while its predecessors (*La Faute de l'abbé Mouret* excepted) were framed in the political context of the Second Empire, *L'Assommoir* broached the much larger social question and testified to the awakening of a man's social conscience. There was indeed abundant justification for Zola's claim that he presented French readers with the first piece of fiction ever devoted to the lower classes, the first that "smelled of the common people," the first that "did not lie." One may well wonder how in heaven some leftist critics found cause to reproach him for slandering the workingman. They missed the clear implication that society at large was responsible, not only for the prosperity of public malefactors such as *père* Colombe, but for the systematic degradation and subjection of the have-nots.

The proletarian "smell" came forth by means of an unheard-of stylistic device. Not content to record conversations in the vernacular, Zola so reported the *thoughts* of his characters. Thus, through a very extraordinary blend of direct and indirect dis-

[21]

course, *L'Assommoir* achieved a consistent "atmospheric" flavor. It did so at considerable risk, if only because slang forms are notoriously ephemeral. Beginning with the title-word itself, which no longer applies in that particular sense, examples of obsolescence have been garnered in an effort to discredit Zola's "philological experiment." The least this writer can say is that, on preparing, thirty-five years ago, a French-English glossary of one chapter of *L'Assommoir,* he found nine-tenths of its vocabulary to be miraculously fresh. Louis-Ferdinand Céline's *Voyage au bout de la nuit* was five years old at the time and already showing symptoms of linguistic arteriosclerosis.

Purists grumbled, mixing their criticism with ideological objections; but the public recovered from initial shock quickly enough to send the book through thirty-five printings in a few months. Unofficially assisted by Zola himself, William Busnach converted Gervaise's story into a melodrama which ran for three hundred consecutive performances. Dance halls echoed to the rhythms of *L'Assommoir-Polka.* Decorative plates representing scenes from the novel were sold at popular prices. First-year royalties enabled the author to purchase, in the suburban village of Médan, on the banks of the Seine, the "rabbit hutch" that was to grow into a somewhat pretentious country-house, a famous literary rendezvous, and, posthumously, the Emile Zola Foundation for sick children of poor families. Fame, wealth, status symbols—all those bourgeois increments abruptly and paradoxically heralded the golden age of Naturalism.

The golden age of Naturalism extended, from *L'Assommoir* to *La Terre,* over a period of exactly ten years (1877–87). This means—well, almost—that it was that of Zola, of *"Zola tout seul,"* as an opponent remarked somewhat later. Whatever following he built never boasted a concerted strategy, let alone a unified doctrine: more about this in a moment. In the last

[22]

analysis, Zola's continued success stemmed from his own ways with the public (if one excepts some unimpressive forays into the theatre) and his consummate skill in throwing the opposition off balance. By far the major part of his strength lay in a bold assessment of what he could accomplish, as a man of letters and would-be indoctrinator, within the frame of bourgeois reference that he felt no need and no urge to subvert. Somewhat different from the Zola of *Mes haines,* the mature Zola chose to trust to the intelligence of the average individual; and alone, it would seem, on the literary scene of his day, he wrote for wide consumption without heaping either flattery or scorn on the heads of his readers. He appointed himself physician extraordinary to a sick society, not its coddler or high executioner. This presupposed, between doctor and client, a bond of confidence and even complicity. The patient must be saved, not only from himself, but from those whose personal or political advantage it was to pronounce him in the best of health; in today's parlance, he must be dissociated from the "Establishment." There was no other meaning to Zola's dictum: "The Republic will be *naturaliste*—or it will not be."

The novelist's popularity reached a new peak in 1880. This, by all odds, should have been his brightest year so far. It was not. As we shall see, private woes descended upon Zola and left him a profoundly disturbed man. Yet, most of the intended harvest was in before the lightning struck—quite enough to make him the master of that particular hour.

1880—the year of *Nana.* As a follow-up to *L'Assommoir* Zola had elected to produce a novel of the "psychological" variety, classically restrained under a romantic title (*Une page d'amour,* volume eight of *Les Rougon-Macquart,* 1878). This, of course, put into effect the grand design he had evolved to keep the critics guessing. Could it be, after all, that M. Zola was no unredeemable blackguard? *Nana* rang out the answer. *Nana* was another "leaf" taken from the Book of Love—but the starkest imaginable, one which divested sexual desire or intercourse of the last shreds of idealization. *Nana* raised (or lowered) Woman to the status of a mythical force, at work to corrupt and disrupt society "between her snow-white thighs." A blind force, by the way, a mere instrument, wholly unconscious of its evil destination. But the instrument of whom—or what? On the one hand, Nana's story provided the true sequel of *L'Assommoir:* not only in the literal sense that the heroine was Gervaise's and Coupeau's daughter, but insofar as she, like her parents, had been preordained from birth to become chattel for the privileged few. Yet, on the other hand, any illustration of that old theme—the Devil and the Flesh—tends to establish man's lust, even the rich man's lust, as a law of nature; willy-nilly, it restricts to hypocrisy, to stuffy righteousness, the guilt of the upper classes. In short, the deterministic system to which Zola was beholden detracted somewhat from the value of *Nana* as a moral and social document. Such as it was, however, the book evoked from the conservative press all the boos its author confidently expected. Reviewers called him an ignoramus (which he *was,* to a large extent, in the ways of profligacy); they branded him an impotent maniac, haunted by unfulfillable erotic dreams. But the public, also as expected, took to *Nana* like fish to water. Only hours after the volume went on sale, its publisher ordered ten thousand copies added to the first printing. Throughout the years, few other works from Zola's pen ever outsold *Nana* in France—and none abroad.

1880—the year of *Les Soirées de Médan.* How many remember today that this collection of six short stories about the Franco-Prussian war, written by Zola and the five young habitués who gathered around his table every Thursday evening, provided the initial vehicle for Maupassant's incomparable *Boule-de-Suif?* The *patron,* for his part, offered *L'Attaque du moulin* (The Attack on the Mill)—a contrived narrative, with ro-

[24]

mantic overtones, which barely overstepped the threshold of honest mediocrity. Nevertheless, the undertaking per se afforded concrete evidence that, for the time being at least, Zola had mustered the loyalties of quite a few promising neophytes. They responded, if truth must be told, to the robustness of his character far more than to his personal brand of aesthetics. Almost to a man, they eschewed complete identification with his "scientific" tenets; but long after they had gone their separate ways, one of them (Huysmans) was heard to exclaim: *"Ah! quels reins* [what loins he has], *ce Zola!"*

1880 — the year of *Le Roman expérimental.* It was yet another "Médanien," Henry Céard, who, in 1879, drew his host's attention to Dr. Claude Bernard's fourteen-year-old *Introduction à l'étude de la médecine expérimentale.* Céard came to rue his initiative, so avidly did Zola take up this little classic and begin appropriating its contents. *Le Roman expérimental* stops short of being a plagiarism only because it professes to be one. The author avowed his intention to "entrench himself" behind Claude Bernard and proceeded to liken the play and interplay of his fictional characters to that of chemical compounds in a test tube. Critic after critic has underscored ever since the childishness of such mechanistic postulates as applied to the workings of literary creation. What should be said in defense of an otherwise indefensible theory is that it was good propaganda. Zola, who flattered himself that he knew how to "drive wedges" into people's minds, had deliberately calculated the impact of this heavy blow. It stamped him in the public eye as the "practical sociologist" he wanted to be.

But 1880 was also a year of mourning. Two losses in succession: that of Flaubert, whom he revered, and that of the elder Mme Zola, threw the novelist into a state of near depression. It took him immense efforts to carry on amid signs that he was prone to morbid fears and mental disturbances. A preoccupation with death — with his own death, final, irremediable, since he no longer expected to have children—crept diffusely into his current work, never to ebb, at least in significant degree, until his liaison with Jeanne Rozerot, from 1888 onwards, rekindled his zest for living and gratified his paternal yearnings. Those intimate adumbrations were to lend unusual color and poignancy to several of his forthcoming novels—not inconsiderably to that which is entitled . . . *La Joie de vivre.*

Conceived in the waning months of 1880, but gestated over a period of years, *La Joie de vivre* did not appear till 1884. It was to have been called "La Douleur," and the dramatic reversal of titles was neither stoically nor sardonically intended. Zola's protagonist, Pauline Quenu, does exemplify the joy of living in the very special sense that she is the lay counterpart to a Sister of Mercy. The daughter of Lisa, the queen of *les Halles,* she has miraculously escaped the curse of heredity or, at any rate, transferred to good deeds, to the renunciation of personal gain, the purposefulness that her mother brought to acquisitive ends. Yet, Pauline, by the very nature of her mission, inhabits a vale of sorrows, just as surely as Alfred de Vigny's Eloa, the angel of compassion, inhabited a world of evil. Thus, *La Joie de vivre,* unique as such in Zola's production, projects the image of a divided man and author, whose humanitarian resolves identify him with his heroine, and his broodings, with the recipients of her charity.

Let no one believe that Zola, unsettled though he was, could remain silent for long. While waiting for *La Joie de vivre* to mature, he added instalments ten and eleven to the *Rougon-Macquart* series. Octave Mouret, abbé Serge's brother, served as a connecting link between *Pot-Bouille* (Steaming Cauldron, 1882) and *Au Bonheur des Dames* (Ladies' Delight, 1883). Throughout the former this ambivalent character assumes a fair share of the petty intrigues and sordid amorous encounters that take place within the walls of an apartment house; in the latter, he presides regally over the management of a department store

[26]

and, on making his first million, proposes marriage to the most devoted (and least corruptible) of his salesgirls. Both works are substandard—for a Zola, that is—but show him still playing cat-and-mouse with the pundits. Whereas *Pot-Bouille* resembled *Nana* in its savage depiction of bourgeois (this time lower middle-class) appetites, its successor sounded like a hymn to free capitalistic enterprise. What kind of a person was this M. Zola, anyway? Hardly had the "troglodytes" given their accolade to the "safe" doctrines embodied in *Au Bonheur des Dames,* than the irrepressible trouble-monger let go of his towering master-piece in the form of a quasi-socialistic novel.

Germinal, Zola's epic of the coal mines, is essentially the story of a strike and of its repression at the hands of the Army. The action is set in 1864—the year when the First International was born; the year, too, when the government of Napoleon III granted French labor the right to strike while denying it the right to organize. This crude formula, an invitation to bloody conflict, or endless litigation, or both, prevailed until March, 1884, at which time the Third Republic extended *de jure* recognition to most labor unions.

March, 1884: note the date. When Zola drew the first sketches of *Germinal,* shortly after the new year, he may have had it in mind to assert the prerogatives of an "experimental" novelist and press for quick adoption of the new law. As it happened, events robbed him of that privilege. Parliament acted under the sting of a long and bitter strike which broke out, on February 21, at the mines of Anzin in northern France. The disturbance, on the other hand, provided Zola with a "live" background, far better suited to his broader purposes than the documentation he had culled—on the subject of labor unrest—from specialized books. He rushed to Anzin, mingled with the miners, inter-viewed managers of the struck companies, even insisted on de-scending into a pit. As a result, the novel throbs with barely suppressed excitement and indignation.

[27]

Yet, it is not a "socialist" novel, at least not in the modern sense of the word. The title itself, borrowed from the revolutionary calendar of 1792, strongly suggests that its ideological roots plunge all the way back into the eighteenth century. Moreover, no little symbolic significance attaches to the fact that 1885, the year of *Germinal*'s unveiling, also was that of Victor Hugo's death and apotheosis. Had Zola planned to don the Old Seer's mantle, his timing could not have been better: for *Germinal* was in effect an updated version of *Les Misérables* — a reminder that, both physically and spiritually, man was born and created to breathe the open air, not the foul vapors of subterranean depths. But nowhere does the writer commit himself to the violent therapeutics of either Proudhon or Karl Marx; nowhere does he uphold the principle of class struggle and advocate a proletarian take-over. There is indeed some evidence that the Paris Commune of 1871 had left a sour taste in his mouth; that his sporadic contacts, through Turgenev, with Russian political refugees (Kropotkin, Bakunin, Lavrov, after whom he fashioned the Souvarine of *Germinal*) increased his abhorrence of radical means; and that his subsequent interview (1886) with Jules Guesde, the French Marxist leader, all but confirmed him in the belief that the "pie-in-the-sky" promises of Socialism were pure demagoguery.

As a warning, however, or as a prophecy, *Germinal* purported to be, and was, and remained ever after, Zola's most solemn utterance in the realm of "practical sociology." It presented the ruling classes with, according to him, an inescapable dilemma: either they would atone for their shameless exploitation of the downtrodden, of those they confined to the level of beasts, or they would sign their own death warrant. Piecemeal legislation —of the "too little and too late" variety—could not possibly prevent the "germination" of a "black and vengeful army" whose explosive potential was more than enough to "blow the earth to bits."

[28]

Germinal surpasses *L'Assommoir* in that it is built on a heroic scale. The spotlight falls no longer on a handful of workingmen, but on the toiling, suffering masses presented as an entity; no longer on their ill-spent idle hours, but on a lifetime bereft of idle hours—unless you count as such the moments they devote to procreating, in mechanical abandon, the galley slaves (or avengers?) of the future. The devouring monster who faces them is no longer a mere alembic, a provider of oblivion, ensconced in a neighborhood tavern; it is the consortium known as the *Régie* (Governing Board), whose decrees, issued in Paris and carried out by local subordinates, resemble those of a remote and implacable deity. By no means does this aggrandizement result in a lack of individual characterization; yet, such is Zola's absolute mastery that personal lives appear to be—indeed are meant to be—submerged within the pulsating, swirling, random life of the whole. The mob scenes for which *Germinal* is justly famous serve to emphasize its emblematic quality. So does the invisibility of the *Régie*. So does the gnawing feeling, implanted on page after page, that both camps, however unevenly, are but the tools of a third force, call it Fate if you will, tortuously engaged in leading mankind, through blood, sweat, and tears, to an unknown destination. *Germinal* has all the features and—so does the author hope—the cleansing power of a Greek tragedy. When the strikers, driven into submission by hunger and rifle-fire, show a disposition to resume work, Souvarine, the dreamy nihilist who until then had cloaked himself in contemptuous aloofness, blows up the mine and floods it. An ambivalent gesture—not in his eyes, to be sure, but from the lofty dialectical standpoint that Zola maintained throughout his career: a trauma is a purge; every night brings promise of the dawn.

Insofar as the wretched miners of *Germinal* had a leader, the part fell to Etienne Lantier, youngest of Gervaise Macquart's illegitimate children. He was cast in the not-too-savory role of a self-taught, youthful militant whose immature notions cannot provide inspired guidance and gradually estrange him from his followers. As he departs for Paris, in a fit of enraged frustration, we are given broad hints that he will sink to the level of raw politics — perhaps become the prototype of the corrupt labor chieftain. This, in our day, might supply the kernel of a resounding, cynical success story. Not so with Zola. In true Darwinian (and puritanical) style, he dooms his inadequate hero to ultimate failure and oblivion. From the family tree one learns that Etienne will participate in the Paris Commune of 1871, be tried, and languish thereafter as a deportee in faraway New Caledonia.

This, in turn, supplies a clue to the meaning of *L'Oeuvre* (The Masterpiece), next to appear in the series (1886). Granted the externals of *L'Oeuvre* thoroughly differed from those of *Germinal.* It was to be the novel of the art world — a world with which Zola was long since conversant; and it was to lay bare the dilemmas of creativeness, many times removed from the so-called social question. Yet, in broad philosophical terms, the new book again raised the social question par excellence: whereto the weary pilgrims of the century? The change of milieu was not so abrupt as appeared at first sight: art, too, had its "Estabishment," its oppressive *Régie,* its angry young men, its crusaders and fumbling pioneers, its traitors and *agents provocateurs.* The moment remained exactly the same: a murky period precariously suspended between past and future, a time for anguish and soul-searching. Moreover, the "race" factor, in *L'Oeuvre,* looms as ominously as ever. Claude Lantier, the main character, is Etienne's flesh-and-blood brother; and far more disinterested, far more appealing though he is, his career, *mutatis mutandis,* follows the same downward path. A painter by vocation, he, too, is largely self-made and plagued with a lack of intellectual discipline which causes him to squander his natural gifts. He, too, has a diseased mind: his pursuit of originality turns to frenzy and impotence and warps his sense of values,

[30]

both human and artistic. He, too, will end in abject failure: not a *raté* in the mediocre sense—rather a near-genius, who either overshot or undershot the mark and, at the time of his self-inflicted death, leaves "nothing of note, absolutely nothing" behind him.

Was Claude's figure drawn in the pseudo-likeness of Manet, or Cézanne, or both? Was he set up as a straw man, the better to burn them in effigy? Speculation has been rife on the subject . . . Quite undeniably, Zola was no longer an ardent admirer and defender of the new school of painting. He still clamored for revolutionary ways of "seeing" and "rendering," still upheld the "regenerators" as regenerators, but questioned, unwisely as now appears, the permanent value of their achievements. In due time he dubbed both Cézanne and Manet "unfulfilled geniuses," with more than a suggestion that Cézanne it was who sinned through exuberance, and Manet through some sort of anemic deficiency. Only to that extent, however, did they (and others, no doubt) pose as models for Claude Lantier. Zola fully exercised the novelist's privilege to extract one composite character from multiple reality. He did not tax his erstwhile friends with pathological tendencies other than those of the century at large—from which he, Zola, considered himself a sufferer just as well. Actually, the more one analyzes Claude's final, abortive "masterpiece"—a nude allegory of Womanhood who rises against a bustling Parisian background, whose haunches and navel are painted a bright vermilion, whose gilded thighs resemble the pillars of an altar, whose genitals flower into a "mystical rose"—the more is one reminded, not of anything that ever came from a contemporary brush, but of the aberrations of decadent Symbolism as shown—a little later—in the literary works of *fin-de-siècle* illuminati.

L'Oeuvre, in fact, is above all else an autobiographical novel—the most "intimate" Zola ever wrote and, as such, quite possibly, the most moving. Not only does it overflow with memories of

[31]

his childhood in Provence and struggling years in Paris, but it documents the spiritual crisis which had opened in 1880 and shaken his aplomb almost to the breaking point. As late as 1886, *L'Oeuvre* instituted a manner of Don Quixote–Sancho Panza, or Eusebius-and-Florestan, dialogue within himself. Ever since *La Confession de Claude,* that very name, Claude, sometimes used by Zola as a nom de plume, had held strange associations with the romantic and, in his eyes, erratic side of his nature. By way, it would seem, of exorcising his demons, he sent Claude Lantier to a calamitous death and camped alongside him the far steadier figure of Pierre Sandoz, a professional writer and the lifelike image of Zola the plodder, of Zola the would-be believer in the "no-nonsense" of science and the virtues of patient endeavor. Yet, the book closes on a very ambiguous note. Standing over Claude's grave, Sandoz chides himself for "cheating with life" as his friend never did: in other terms, for issuing under false pretenses works which he knows in his heart of hearts are no more authentic and viable than Lantier's own compositions. Were this to be accepted literally, Sandoz's abrupt resolve *(allons travailler!)* would sound very hollow indeed, and *L'Oeuvre* might be called a bleak admission of failure on the part of Zola the poet *and* Zola the scientist.

As it happened, the fortunes of both took an unexpected turn. The romantic demons had not been exorcised after all. They returned in full fury and, more surprisingly still, they, not Sandoz's sedate gods, pointed the way to ultimate liberation. Ostensibly *La Terre* (Earth, 1887) was to forge another link — the fifteenth — in a long chain of "experiments." Today, however, with the benefit of hindsight, we realize that this controversial work, in fact and in effect, broke the pseudo-scientific spell under which the novelist had been laboring for years.

The sociological intent of *La Terre* was indeed obscure. Although one episodic character could be heard advocating agrarian socialism, by no means did he propound the author's views.

[32]

Farmers, even the more substantial among them, were shown to suffer from a variety of economic ills; but Zola appeared to be reasonably satisfied that they themselves bore a measure of responsibility for their plight. Briefly, the peasants, unlike industrial workers, were one of the oldest social classes in existence; they stood within reach of the ancestral dream—ownership of the land; yet, having thrown off the shackles of serfdom, they remained slaves to the flinty qualities which had won the struggle for them—their rapaciousness, their guile, their insatiable animal hunger. One would hesitate to say that Zola felt out of sympathy with the peasantry, but it must be admitted that his saga of the countryside breathed none of the warmth, and little of the urgency, which not so long ago pervaded the pages of *Germinal.* Despite the fact that the novelist went through his usual paces, revisiting his mother's native Beauce for on-the-spot documentation, the suspicion arises that the end product, qua novel, was primarily a rhetorical exercise based upon literary reminiscences. It was meant to relegate to their proper place the bucolic fantasies of George Sand—and in this it succeeded admirably. It also invited comparison with Balzac whose unfinished fresco, *Les Paysans,* bid fair to count among his greatest: perhaps a good enough reason why this direct challenge to an awesome predecessor lacked the imaginative power which Zola had brought or would bring to several others. As an observer of the rural scene he contributed little that was intrinsically new and seemed content to accentuate Balzacian traits. From Fourchon to Fouan, from Courtecuisse to Bécu or Lequeu, from Mouche to Mouche (pure coincidence?), family names retained their punlike, sometimes half-obscene quality. Greed and murderous hatred, not to mention uninhibited lust, supplied the main motivations as they had done in *Les Paysans*—only more so. Cunning remained the peasant's favorite weapon, but violence, already present in Balzac, was markedly on the increase. Comic relief turned to positive ribaldry. Where Balzac

[33]

had made a wry jumble of human and animal life on the farm, Zola pointedly juxtaposed the insemination of cows and that of women, or again the birth of a calf and that of a child.

Harsh though it may sound, this estimate of *La Terre* does not purport to exonerate its original detractors. The work should have been recognized for what it was, for what the author intuitively felt it to be: "the living poem of the soil"; or, more accurately perhaps, the poem of man's incestuous attachment to the earth. The poem of Cybele as mother and mistress: equally demanding in both roles, yet strangely sparing at times, or at least capricious, in the dispensation of her bounties. A poem as removed from the paradisiacal climate of the Paradou garden as reality can be from a midsummer night's dream. The poem of fecundity, yes, but of fecundity through human fecundation. The earth's womb must be penetrated, the seed sown, the fruit reaped; men must sweat and men must die, so that "the bread of life may spring from the land." In this respect at any rate, *La Terre* far outdistanced Balzac's conceptions. Out of its manure-scented chapters there issued, willy-nilly, a paean to civilization: for, no matter how close to the brute man was depicted to be, he was also credited with a dim sense of direction and purposefulness. But for him the planet would forever remain a desert or a jungle.

La Terre proved to be another popular success—probably for the wrong reasons. It did portend, however, profound changes in Zola's status within the literary world. The first blow, a painful one no doubt, came from the ranks. Editorialized by *Figaro* on August 18, 1887, the famous "Manifeste des Cinq" violently upbraided Zola's "betrayal," his "descent into unadulterated filth," and the "Hugoesque inflation" which robbed his characters of any credibility. The five young signatories were of course not the Médan habitués, but they had been fellow travelers up to that point; they were, to be exact, followers of Alphonse

Daudet and Edmond de Goncourt, who, out of sheer jealousy, either inspired their diatribe or secretly chuckled over it; and it may well be that, as a result of their action, the Médaniens themselves felt badly shaken. *La Terre* caused to explode, not only an accumulation of petty rancors, but the intellectual differences which separated Zola from even his most loyal retinue. Always tenuous at best, Naturalist "unity" fell to pieces within the space of a few years. Meanwhile conservative critics, ever on the lookout for a chink in Zola's armor, had pounced on their long-awaited opportunity. Less than two weeks after the publication of the "Manifeste des Cinq," Ferdinand Brunetière, official spokesman for the *Revue des Deux Mondes,* was blazoning the fact that "the master had finally alienated his disciples" and proclaiming *urbi et orbi* "the bankruptcy of Naturalism."

It is entirely conceivable that the threatened dispersal of Naturalism did not displease Zola altogether. Let his opponents cry havoc as long as the general public stayed solidly and unquestioningly behind him. (It did. Not even the utter chastity of his next book, *Le Rêve,* almost perverse in its contrast to *La Terre,* could disconcert and discourage his readers.) Furthermore, let Naturalism disintegrate if it must and if the net result should be a sense of emancipation he, Zola, had come to crave as much as anyone else. The day was approaching when he would assume a sanguine mood and offer himself as a . . . valedictorian for the whole movement. The future, he prophesied (to Jules Huret in 1891),

belongs to the man or men who will plumb the soul of modern society; who, having rid themselves of excessively rigid doctrines, will prove amenable to a more plausible, softer-hearted acceptance of life. I am looking forward to a broader, more complex representation of the truth, to greater openness in our understanding of mankind, to, shall we say, a classical coming of age of Naturalism.

[35]

Whereupon, the same reporter tells us, his buoyant inter-locutor had blurted out: "And mind you, if I live long enough, I'll do them myself—the things *they* want!"

Whence this truculent exercise in benignity? whence this new upsurge of self-confidence? By the time of the Huret interview, few were those, among Zola's acquaintances, who did not know or suspect the answer. Mme Zola herself was about to learn that, ever since the last months of 1888, her husband had been carry-ing on an affair with her former seamstress, Jeanne Rozerot, an attractive and reasonably literate girl in her early twenties. Originally at least, the aging novelist had fallen prey to what he himself described as a "recrudescence of life"—to what his contemporary, Paul Bourget, aptly called "the demon of twelve-noon"; but, as we know, there was nothing in him of the prof-ligate, nor was Jeanne a sordid adventuress. Their attachment became unbreakable when she bore him a daughter and a son. Over and above his pangs of remorse Zola's paternal pride led him to profess a renewed ability to "move mountains." He weathered his wife's anger, which relented only at length and then solely for the sake of the children. Not the least of a number of ironical twists was that being a father—even out of wedlock— gave him an added sense of bourgeois respectability. He now had a stake in the future. Yesterday the ribbon of the Legion of Honor; tomorrow—why not—a seat in the French Academy: and would M. Brunetière be red in the face! Membership in the Academy never materialized, but what matters to posterity is that the dialogue between life and death which ran steadily through Zola's novels no longer was allowed to end on a note of despair.

As might be expected, this shift in inspirational values did not occur overnight. It was, in fact, to follow a jagged course through the remaining volumes of *Les Rougon-Macquart. Le Rêve* (The Dream, 1888), a romantic idyl and perhaps some-thing more: perhaps a spiritual purge in the aftermath of *La*

[36]

Terre, antedates Zola's liaison; yet, it coincides with his first "dreams" of amorous rejuvenation and must have assumed, in retrospect, a premonitory character: for, of its several drafts, one took up the ancient theme of the senescent guardian falling helplessly in love with his ward. *La Bête humaine* (The Beast in Man, 1890), on the other hand, and, to a lesser extent, *L'Argent* (Money, 1891) testify to the stubbornness of old habits. Only in *La Débâcle* (1892) and *Le Docteur Pascal* (1893) did Zola's new (or renewed) gospel sound loud and clear.

With the world of railroads as its background, *La Bête humaine* bid fair, and indeed purported, to be still another probe into the scope and meaning of material progress. As a devotee of science, Zola could ill afford not to celebrate the wonders of the railroad track and its contribution to "the exchange of ideas, the transformation of nations, the mingling of races, the ultimate unification of the planet." Yet, he chose (was it a choice? was it not, rather, a kind of compulsion?) to underline the mechanical or mechanizing aspects of technological advance. There is a futuristic coloring to his vision of Jacques Lantier, the engineer, grafted, so to speak, onto his engine, *la Lison,* as one with her in a vertiginous sexual embrace. It is, however, an unequal and darkly symbolic embrace. The life of the machine suffuses that of the man, empties his mind of whatever rational processes may have been his, restores him to his feral origins. Thus, the story evolves into a recital of wanton crime and bloody murder. It goes even farther than did *La Terre* in stressing the animality of man: for, whereas the epic of the fields found a layer of civilization deeply embedded within the human beast, that of the railroads exposes the human beast under a thin crust of civilization.

Through the expedient of returning Saccard, the protagonist of *La Curée,* to the center of the stage, Zola presumed to open to his readers the *sanctum sanctorum* of modern capitalism—namely, the stock market. A rash venture on his part, since he knew nothing of its operations, never owned a share in his life, never even possessed a bank account. The true wonder, then, is not that *L'Argent* should fall far short of being a masterpiece, but that it should be as competent a novel as it actually is. Zola's informants did their homework: with the result that, structural weaknesses notwithstanding, *L'Argent* today remains unrivaled as a portrayal of the Stock Exchange and would need few transpositions to evoke for us, not the distant saga of speculation under the Second Empire, but that, closer to our times, of the Staviskys in France or the Insulls in America. Saccard's financial schemes, as well may be imagined, come to a crash in a kind of *Götterdämmerung* atmosphere, with hosts of hapless victims left wailing across the night. Yet, surprisingly enough, Zola does not issue a blanket indictment of his hero. Saccard's recklessness is taken to be but a malformation or misuse of the creative urge that makes the world go round. Not a little sophistry attaches to this judgment whose devious purpose it is to bring out an analogy with love. Money has no odor; money is what money manipulators make it. Likewise—and this is a note not heard in Zola's novels since *La Faute de l'abbé Mouret*—none of the filth that is being stirred in the name of love can defile love itself.

Should war, both foreign and civil, be defended, or excused, on roughly the same dialectical grounds? Should we look upon it as an illustration of Darwin's "haughty and heart-rending" law of necessity—then make a text and pretext of that very premise to assert: "War is life itself. . . . None but the warlike nations ever prospered. A nation perishes the minute it disarms"? This was the tenor of a Zola article published in *Figaro* on the twenty-first anniversary of the Sedan capitulation and generally considered to be a "blurb" for his forthcoming novel, *La Débâcle*. Not long ago, this article and the novel itself came under heavy criticism from an otherwise very sympathetic commentator, Henri Guillemin, who sees in them a damaging concession to the "Establishment" (remember: Zola coveted a seat in the French Academy!) and a whitewashing of the retrograde policies followed after Sedan—up to and including the savage repression of the Commune uprising. We shall, in these pages, adopt a kindlier view of Zola's motivations. We made it clear that he had a flair for publicity and was not above making opportunistic moves. We also took note of the fact that, while his heart beat to the left, his head tended to lean to the right in vague fear of the "red peril" that somehow the writing of *Germinal* had conjured up before his eyes. It is no less true, however, that he had been toiling for twenty-five years on the fundamental assumption that his appointed task was to cleanse the Augean stables *of the Second Empire.* For twenty of those twenty-five years he had regarded Sedan as a deed of immanent justice which closed an era and opened another. What he wrote in 1891 he could have written in 1871 just as well—that Sedan was relevant, "not merely in terms of war," but also and chiefly as "the collapse of a dynasty and the tumbling down of an age." How, then, could he, without tearing up the fabric of his work, without repudiating its conclusions, acknowledge publicly—whether or not he acknowledged privately—that nothing was changed and not even the trauma of Sedan had been able to raise France from the trough of corruption? Short of becoming an out-and-out revolutionary, the author of *Les Rougon-Macquart* was bound to express temporary faith in the Third Republic and long-term confidence in the due process of evolution. Thus *La Débâcle* will reintone the litanies so often encountered in earlier novels— only magnified by the euphoria of new-found love and parenthood. Over the Sedan holocaust, over Paris still ablaze in the wake of fratricidal war, an immaculate sky keeps singing "of eternal nature, of eternal humanity," of "the renewal promised to all who hope and who labor."

By no means an impeccably constructed novel, *La Débâcle* stands nevertheless as one of Zola's most impressive achievements. It is a work of great scope and power, not unworthy of comparison with Tolstoy's *War and Peace.* Sweepingly majestic in its description of the battlefields, crystal-clear in its reconstruction of strategic or tactical maneuvers, masterly in its handling of enormous masses of men, it shows Zola at his narrative and epic best. Yet, the emphasis appears to be on individuals, combatants and noncombatants alike. There is merit in the author's later boast that he discarded, once and for all, the trappings, the flourishes, the heroics of the conventional war tale, substituting for them the naked truth: that of the smoke, the noise, the bloodshed, the stench, the pent-up brutality, the visceral fears, the cries of the wounded, the involvement of innocent bystanders—civilians, women, children. This may be the reason why, at a time when the Franco-Prussian war (and the Commune) remained very much a topical subject, when veterans were just about reaching the reminiscent age, the success of *La Débâcle*—Zola's best-seller ever—exceeded all expectations. This may also be the reason why the Army took a dim view of it. One prominent general averred that he was "shocked"; another chided the author for presenting reality "under noxious aspects." No better proof is needed that, if perchance Zola tried appeasing the "Establishment," part at least of the Establishment refused the bait—thus setting the stage for the open break that was to be precipitated by the Dreyfus Affair.

To all practical or hopefully practical purposes, then, the "debacle" of the imperial regime signaled that of the Rougon-Macquart tribe, so that the nineteenth book of the series brought it to its logical end. Since, however, in keeping with Zola's philosophy, every end calls for a beginning, the twentieth and last volume would provide that beginning. We have already given proper consideration to the recapitulative aspects of *Le Docteur Pascal* and should be content at this time to lay stress on the strong emotional impulse which made it a thinly veiled

[40]

transposition of Zola's personal love story. Pascal Rougon "weds" his niece, Clotilde (without benefit of clergy), and has a child by her. That, unlike Zola, he had been a lifelong bachelor removes from him the "stigma" of adultery; that he is at least ten years older than his creator when he becomes a father accentuates further, not indeed the incongruity of his "marriage," but, on the contrary, its Ruth-and-Boaz quality, the symbolic beauty, the invincible promise, the sanctity of it. To Van Salten Kolff, February 22, 1893:

I thought it was courageous, on concluding this history of the terrible Rougon-Macquart family, to have it give birth to a last child: the unknown child, perhaps the Messiah of tomorrow. A mother nursing her child, isn't that continuing the world—and redeeming it?

As it happened, Zola did not wait for the Messiah of tomorrow. Almost two full years before finishing *Les Rougon-Macquart*, shortly after the Huret interview of 1891, he set out to "rid himself of excessively rigid doctrines" and achieve "greater openness in [his] understanding of mankind." This was tantamount to instituting himself the Messiah of today.

In a sense he had never been anything else. To show his true colors as a kindred spirit to the Hugos and the Michelets, all he had to do was throw away the paraphernalia of the "experimental novel" and pick up the pilgrim's staff which had lain within reach in a corner of his laboratory. What is more, *Le Docteur Pascal* made it clear that this could be done without renouncing one's scientific tenets: it was just a matter of endowing modern technology and modern economics with a spirituality of their own. The conflict between science and religion, between progressive and traditional values, would be resolved through a return to fundamentals. Universal love: not only human brotherhood, but a St. Francis-like extension of it to every living thing, would eventually lead to universal peace and harmony. In a world whose inexhaustible bounties could be rationally devel-

[41]

oped and distributed, even the Darwinian concepts upheld in *La Débâcle* would lose their dire pertinence. Zola saw no contradiction between his tolerance of war as a means of surgical purification—when the tree is diseased and the rotten branch must be cut off—and his advocacy of nonviolence in a society pure and mature enough to turn its technical knowledge into an instrument of social justice. He, not unlike Tolstoy, acquired the conviction that, by divesting the New Testament of its supernatural envelope, by breaking the Church's monopoly over it, one could extract from its teachings the charter of the future. And, again not unlike Tolstoy, he saw the artist as the apostle of the new faith. As if in anticipation of André Gide's famous axiom that good feelings make for bad literature, he, in the last decade of his life, endeavored to prove exactly the opposite.

Alas, he did not succeed. There are, to be sure, passages of great force and brilliance in Zola's triptych, *Les Trois villes* ([The Three Cities]: *Lourdes,* 1894; *Rome,* 1896; *Paris,* 1898), and in the unfinished "Four Gospels" (*Les Quatre Evangiles: Fécondité,* 1899; *Travail,* 1901; *Vérité,* posthumous, 1903; the fourth, *Justice,* was never written). This enormous production, however, while it bears witness to the author's unflagging stamina, is decidedly anticlimactic from a literary standpoint. It takes uncommon courage to follow abbé Pierre Froment's spiritual journey from Lourdes, the shrine of "naive faith and illusion"—through Rome, the hardheaded metropolis of political Catholicism—to Paris, where he finally resolves to abandon his cassock and become a lay worker in the service of justice and human love. Of the three novels involved, the least unrewarding is probably *Paris,* if only because a certain grandeur attaches to the implicit contrast between the Paris of the Rougon-Macquart era and the new Paris of the coming century, hopefully reinstated in its former role as the capital of Thought. But then nothing less than heroism is required to withstand the heavy rhetoric, the utopian arbitrariness, the utter unreality of Zola's

[42]

Evangiles. Even their symbolism descends at times to sheer puerility: the "Gospels" were to unfold the life story of Pierre Froment's four sons, pointedly christened Mathieu, Luc, Marc, and Jean after the four Evangelists; the patronymic itself, Froment (*wheat* in French), becomes an obvious emblem of fertility; Mathieu's wife, Marianne, borrows her given name from the girl in the Phrygian cap who traditionally personifies the French Republic; and that happy couple gives birth to twelve children who in turn present it, on its diamond wedding anniversary, with one hundred and thirty-four grandchildren and great-grandchildren. Were it not for lack of space, we might be tempted to probe more deeply into the whys and wherefores of Zola's messianic intemperance; we might even reach some instructive and not altogether damning conclusions; yet, one of them would have to be that, if *La Débâcle* came reasonably close to emulating Tolstoy's *War and Peace,* none of Zola's subsequent works even remotely offers itself as a counterpart to *Resurrection.*

If we are to believe Alphonse Daudet—but *is* Daudet believable?—Zola's irruption into the Dreyfus case was primarily due to his fondness for the limelight. This would be presupposing that he himself was aware of a decline in his creative powers and anxious to divert his energies into other than literary channels. The inference would also be that, for the first time in years, he grievously misjudged public reaction. As a result of his gesture, his popularity faded overnight, never to return in full panoply until long after his death.

Reasons for this are not far to seek. For many months after Captain Alfred Dreyfus was found guilty of treasonable acts (December 22, 1894) and deported to Devil's Island, few if any outside his family challenged the verdict. Still stung by her defeats, the nation at large was riding a wave of jingoism which made the Army—or its decisions—virtually untouchable. Then Dreyfus was a Jew. The image of the Jews as an "alien" element,

bent on capturing all control wheels and subverting all traditional values—that image was being successfully kept in the
forefront of public consciousness by the likes of Edouard Dru-
ment, the venomous author of *La France juive* (1886), whose
newspaper, *La Libre Parole,* had been founded for the express
purpose of spreading the anti-Semitic creed. So it is that when
Zola, long before becoming interested in the Dreyfus case per
se, rose in defense of the Jews (*Pour les Juifs, Figaro,* May 16,
1896), he was already contradicting the prevalent mood and
aligning himself with the fractious, "intellectual," minority.

Only the salient facts about Zola's intervention and subsequent trial—this affair within an affair—may be recalled here.
Late in 1897, when the finger of evidence began pointing away
from Dreyfus and to a fellow officer, Major Esterhazy; when
the latter was forced to request a hearing, ostensibly to "clear
his name," Zola, through a series of articles and brochures,
joined in the demand for a review of the Dreyfus sentence.
Esterhazy's swift acquittal by a court-martial (January 11, 1898)
effectively squashed this move and prompted Zola to write his
impassioned *Lettre à M. Félix Faure, Président de la Répu-
blique.* Published January 13 in Georges Clemenceau's *L'Aurore,*
known to posterity under the title, *J'accuse,* which Clemenceau
gave it, this "letter" inculpated the entire military hierarchy—
here and there somewhat randomly for lack of adequate proof,
but with unerring accuracy in its over-all assumption that the
Army was concealing its mistakes and saving face at the expense
of common justice. A libel suit, instituted by the government,
inevitably followed, and Zola was condemned to the maximum
penalty of one year in prison and a 3,000-franc fine (February
23). Having lost on appeal (July 18), he was prevailed upon,
by Clemenceau and others, to evade the sentence—on the
grounds, it would seem, that this was the only way to keep the
Dreyfus case open. A reluctant Zola stole away to England and
remained there until June of the following year, when he was

still technically liable to arrest but the march of events made it fairly safe for him to return. In his absence the tangled truth had begun unraveling: a high officer had committed suicide; Esterhazy had fled and issued from abroad a confession of sorts; orders were going out to bring Dreyfus back for a retrial. As he stepped on French soil, Zola called his homecoming "a rebirth" and the results of his campaign "a harvest of uprightness, equity, and infinite hope."

It did not take him long to realize how mistaken he was. Unable to exonerate Dreyfus without incriminating senior officers, the military court chose to recondemn him . . . with extenuating circumstances! He who should have been acquitted was awarded instead a magnanimous presidential "pardon." The "Dreyfus crusade" fizzled out—partly because Dreyfus himself, an Army man whose mental processes did not basically differ from those of his accusers, chose to discourage it and wait six more years for his total rehabilitation (July 15, 1906). Meanwhile, an amnesty bill designed to liquidate the Affair as expediently as possible was rammed through Parliament and defended by the Premier, Waldeck-Rousseau, in the crudest terms imaginable: "Amnesty," he said, "does not judge, does not accuse, does not acquit: it ignores." Last-minute "Dreyfusists" prepared to make hay out of the labors of early "Dreyfusards." Young Charles Péguy complained mournfully that "every mystique degenerates into politics."

Zola, for his part, went on fighting. *La Vérité en marche* (Truth on the March, 1901), a collection of his writings throughout the Dreyfus Affair, contains—apropos of the "pardon" and on the subject of amnesty—vigorous protests against the guileful policies followed by the government. There can be no question, however, that Zola's former assertive tones ("Dreyfus is innocent. I swear it. I pledge my life. I pledge my honor. . . . I may be smitten here, [but] I shall conquer . . .") were giving way to those of disbelief and frustration: "I stand in dread . . .

[45]

in sacred terror. . . . The impossible [has] come to pass. . . . Future generations will shudder in shame," etc. A veteran of many journalistic brawls, but a novice in the field of action, Zola was visibly shaken. Indomitable, yet shaken. Mud-slinging and derision had taken their toll:

> Zola's a big pig,
> The older he gets, the stupider he is;
> Zola's a big pig,
> Let's catch and roast the silly pig.

He had earned the suffrage of part at least of the intelligentsia; a book of homage had been presented to him (1898) under the patronage of a Franco-Belgian committee which included, besides Clemenceau, Maurice Maeterlinck and Emile Verhaeren; but the first words of dedication read—all too ominously: "The people learn their lesson even as they lapidate who loves them."

The posturing, the prophesying, the anathematizing—and the resultant lapidation—were part and parcel of the romantic heritage which Zola, wisely or not, had chosen to assume in later years. After half a century or so he was reechoing Hugo's hyperbolic claim that he would scale the heavens in order to steal the truth; that, if thunders should bark, *he* would roar. Whatever megalomania is involved here may be a character trait—it certainly was in Hugo's case; but its deeper significance must be assessed in the context of romantic vaticination. Sooner or later, with Hugo and Zola, there comes a time when the man subsumes himself into the poet; when his commitment to self-expression reaches the visionary level; when the word becomes the Word in so spontaneous a manner that even self-conceit acquires the colors of self-abnegation. It is, I believe, extremely revealing that Zola should have sworn to Dreyfus's innocence "by my forty years of toil, by the authority that such labor may have given me." This is at once romantic nonsense and the reason why Zola's championship of Dreyfus is still remembered, whereas

[46]

other participants in the drama, including Dreyfus himself, are readily forgotten. Let us face it: we went, we are still going, through experiences which dwarf the Dreyfus case; Zola's involvement in the specific issues thereof has, really, no greater relevance to our times than Voltaire's effort on behalf of Calas; but what matters in modern terms is that he entered the fray, not as a high-minded politician (assuming the breed exists), not as a man of action, not even as a writer systematically *engagé* in the Sartrean sense of the word, but as a *clerc* (Julien Benda's expression), *as a man of thought,* whose devotion to principles, and to principles only, prepared, nay, designated him for this extraordinary assumption of risk and responsibility.

Zola died a strange accidental death, on September 29, 1902, when carbon monoxide fumes issuing from a defective chimney asphyxiated him in his sleep. Talk of foul play arose immediately and is still being intermittently revived. There is little evidence to support it—the most likely explanation being that Zola fell a victim to ingrained, unhealthy habits of another age that some of us are old enough to remember: lighting coal fires in the bedroom—closing windows hermetically—bolting inside doors for added privacy. The sensational aspects of that death lay much less in its manner than in its timing at the hands of Fate. In one of the most eloquent and substantial tributes that the event elicited (there were many hollow ones), Gabriel Trarieux had this to say:

He died at the top of his strength, his faculties still unimpaired. Among all ways of dying this is one to be envied. There are those who deplore that he was denied well-earned returns, a happy old age, the inevitable apotheosis, the vast emotional outpouring which took place, on a starry Spring night, around the peaceful coffin of Victor Hugo. Of small importance, however, in the face of the gestures of survivors. I, for one, am of the opinion that the style of his funeral—which was his last battle—suited best that incorrigible warrior, far too bitterly dedicated ever to become a patriarch. Clashing hurrahs and outrages are an apotheosis, too, and the proof that one still lives. This kind of an apotheosis Hugo also would have known if he had died on the morrow of his *Châtiments.*

[47]

A SHORT BIBLIOGRAPHICAL NOTE

The standard edition of Zola's *Oeuvres completes* is that published by Charpentier-Fasquelle (48 vols.). The limited Bernouard edition (1927–29, 50 vols.), with notes and commentaries by Maurice Le Blond, Zola's son-in-law, is no longer readily available. A far richer and truly critical edition in 15 vols. (Paris, Cercle du Livre Précieux) is currently nearing completion under the direction of Henri Mitterand.

The *Rougon-Macquart* cycle of twenty novels is separately available in the "Bibliothèque de la Pléiade" (Gallimard, 5 vols.). Its critical apparatus, also by Henri Mitterand, is an indispensable tool for researchers.

Older translations into English, especially those by E. A. Vizitelly, are bowdlerized and unreliable. Among the recent ones the following will be found more or less satisfactory:

Thérèse Raquin, 1962; *L'Assommoir,* 1970; *Germinal,* 1954, by L. W. Tancock (Harmondsworth, Middlesex, and Baltimore, Penguin Books);

The Kill (La Curée), 1957, by A. Teixera de Mattos; *Zest for Life (La Joie de vivre),* 1955, by Jean Stewart; *The Masterpiece (L'Oeuvre),* 1950, by Th. Walton; *Earth (La Terre),* 1954, by Ann Lindsay; *The Debacle,* 1968, by John Hands (London, Elek Books);

L'Assommoir, 1962, by Atwood H. Townsend; *Germinal,* 1970, by Stanley and Eleanor Hochman (New York, New American Library);

Nana, 1964, by Lowel Bair (New York, Bantam Books).

A short but very well conceived anthology in translation was contributed by Philip Walker to the collection "Profiles in Literature" (London, Routledge and Kegan Paul, 1969). By far the outstanding biographical and critical study in English, also one of the best in any language, is that by F. W. J. Hemmings (Oxford, The Clarendon Press, 1953; rev. ed., 1966, especially recommended). Also valuable is Elliott M. Grant's monograph (New York, Twayne Publishers, 1966). All three of the above-mentioned works include bibliographies which may be used as a guide through the maze of critical studies extant in the French language.